# 50 Ocean-Friendly Cooking Recipes

By: Kelly Johnson

## Table of Contents

- Grilled Salmon with Lemon Herb Sauce
- Seared Scallops with Garlic Butter
- Miso-Glazed Cod
- Shrimp Tacos with Avocado Salsa
- Baked Trout with Dill and Lemon
- Tuna Poke Bowl
- Fish and Chips with a Healthy Twist
- Grilled Swordfish with Mango Salsa
- Salmon Burger with Spicy Aioli
- Baked Cod with Cherry Tomatoes
- Shrimp Stir-Fry with Vegetables
- Sushi Rolls with Sustainable Fish
- Octopus Salad with Olive Oil and Lemon
- Fish Tacos with Cabbage Slaw
- Grilled Mahi-Mahi with Pineapple Salsa
- Seaweed Salad with Sesame Dressing
- Salmon and Avocado Sushi Bowls
- Shrimp and Zucchini Noodles
- Baked Salmon with Mustard and Herb Crust
- Fish Stew with Fresh Tomatoes
- Sea Bass with Roasted Vegetables
- Grilled Shrimp Skewers with Garlic and Lemon
- Spicy Tuna Salad
- Mackerel with Roasted Potatoes and Kale
- Coconut-Curry Fish Stew
- Poke Salad with Ahi Tuna
- Blackened Tilapia with Avocado
- Grilled Sardines with Garlic and Lemon
- Baked Halibut with Pesto and Cherry Tomatoes
- Mussels in White Wine Sauce
- Shrimp Scampi with Whole Wheat Pasta
- Salmon with Quinoa and Roasted Veggies
- Fish Tacos with Cilantro Lime Dressing
- Seared Tuna with Cucumber and Sesame
- Clam Chowder with a Healthy Twist

- Grilled Salmon with Roasted Asparagus
- Pappardelle with Clams and Garlic
- Baked Fish with Herb-Crusted Potatoes
- Crab Cakes with Lemon-Dijon Aioli
- Sautéed Fish with Zucchini and Tomatoes
- Salmon and Avocado Salad
- Grilled Squid with Lemon and Parsley
- Shrimp and Mango Salad
- Fish Curry with Coconut Milk
- Tuna Salad with Olive Oil and Lemon
- Shrimp and Broccoli Stir-Fry
- Grilled Fish with Herb Chimichurri
- Roasted Sea Bass with Lemon and Capers
- Coconut Shrimp with Sweet Chili Sauce
- Grilled Halibut with Lemon Butter Sauce

**Grilled Salmon with Lemon Herb Sauce**

**Ingredients:**

- 4 salmon fillets
- 2 tablespoons olive oil
- 1 lemon, sliced
- 2 cloves garlic, minced
- 1 teaspoon fresh thyme, chopped
- 1 teaspoon fresh rosemary, chopped
- Salt and pepper to taste
- Fresh parsley for garnish

**Instructions:**

1. **Prepare the Salmon:**
    - Preheat the grill to medium-high heat. Brush salmon fillets with olive oil and season with salt and pepper.
2. **Make the Lemon Herb Sauce:**
    - In a small bowl, mix garlic, lemon slices, thyme, rosemary, and a pinch of salt.
3. **Grill the Salmon:**
    - Grill the salmon for 4-5 minutes per side, or until it flakes easily with a fork.
4. **Serve:**
    - Top with lemon herb sauce and fresh parsley. Serve immediately.

**Seared Scallops with Garlic Butter**

**Ingredients:**

- 12 large scallops, patted dry
- 2 tablespoons olive oil
- 2 tablespoons butter
- 2 cloves garlic, minced
- Salt and pepper to taste
- Fresh parsley for garnish
- Lemon wedges for serving

**Instructions:**

1. **Prepare the Scallops:**
    - Season scallops with salt and pepper. Heat olive oil in a skillet over medium-high heat.
2. **Sear the Scallops:**
    - Add scallops to the skillet and cook for 2-3 minutes per side until golden brown and opaque.
3. **Make the Garlic Butter:**
    - In the same skillet, melt butter and sauté garlic for 1 minute until fragrant.
4. **Serve:**
    - Drizzle garlic butter over scallops, garnish with parsley, and serve with lemon wedges.

**Miso-Glazed Cod**

**Ingredients:**

- 4 cod fillets
- 2 tablespoons miso paste
- 2 tablespoons soy sauce
- 1 tablespoon honey
- 1 tablespoon rice vinegar
- 1 teaspoon sesame oil
- 1 teaspoon grated ginger
- Sesame seeds for garnish
- Green onions, chopped, for garnish

**Instructions:**

1. **Make the Miso Glaze:**
    - In a bowl, whisk together miso paste, soy sauce, honey, rice vinegar, sesame oil, and grated ginger.
2. **Prepare the Cod:**
    - Preheat the oven to 400°F (200°C). Place cod fillets on a baking sheet lined with parchment paper.
3. **Glaze the Cod:**
    - Brush the cod fillets with the miso glaze, reserving a little for drizzling.
4. **Bake the Cod:**
    - Bake for 12-15 minutes, until the cod is opaque and flakes easily.
5. **Serve:**
    - Drizzle with the reserved glaze and garnish with sesame seeds and green onions.

**Shrimp Tacos with Avocado Salsa**

## Ingredients:

- 1 lb shrimp, peeled and deveined
- 1 tablespoon olive oil
- 1 teaspoon chili powder
- 1 teaspoon cumin
- Salt and pepper to taste
- 8 small corn tortillas
- 1 avocado, diced
- 1/2 cup red onion, diced
- 1/4 cup cilantro, chopped
- 1 lime, juiced

## Instructions:

1. **Cook the Shrimp:**
   - Heat olive oil in a skillet over medium-high heat. Season shrimp with chili powder, cumin, salt, and pepper. Cook for 2-3 minutes per side until pink and cooked through.
2. **Make the Avocado Salsa:**
   - In a bowl, combine diced avocado, red onion, cilantro, and lime juice. Season with salt and pepper.
3. **Assemble the Tacos:**
   - Warm the tortillas. Fill each with shrimp and top with avocado salsa.
4. **Serve:**
   - Serve immediately, garnished with extra cilantro if desired.

**Baked Trout with Dill and Lemon**

**Ingredients:**

- 4 trout fillets
- 1 lemon, thinly sliced
- 2 tablespoons olive oil
- 1 tablespoon fresh dill, chopped
- Salt and pepper to taste

**Instructions:**

1. **Prepare the Trout:**
    - Preheat the oven to 375°F (190°C). Place trout fillets on a baking sheet lined with parchment paper.
2. **Season the Trout:**
    - Drizzle olive oil over the fillets and top with lemon slices. Sprinkle with dill, salt, and pepper.
3. **Bake the Trout:**
    - Bake for 12-15 minutes, until the trout is opaque and flakes easily.
4. **Serve:**
    - Serve the trout with additional lemon slices and a garnish of fresh dill.

**Tuna Poke Bowl**

**Ingredients:**

- 1 lb sushi-grade tuna, cubed
- 1/4 cup soy sauce
- 1 tablespoon sesame oil
- 1 tablespoon rice vinegar
- 1 teaspoon honey
- 1 teaspoon grated ginger
- 1 cup cooked rice (white or brown)
- 1/2 cucumber, sliced
- 1/2 avocado, sliced
- 1/4 cup edamame
- 1 tablespoon sesame seeds
- Green onions, chopped, for garnish

**Instructions:**

1. **Marinate the Tuna:**
    - In a bowl, whisk together soy sauce, sesame oil, rice vinegar, honey, and grated ginger. Add tuna cubes and marinate for 10-15 minutes.
2. **Assemble the Bowl:**
    - Divide cooked rice between bowls. Top with marinated tuna, cucumber, avocado, edamame, and sesame seeds.
3. **Serve:**
    - Garnish with green onions and serve immediately.

## Fish and Chips with a Healthy Twist

### Ingredients:

- 4 white fish fillets (such as cod or haddock)
- 1 cup whole wheat flour
- 1 teaspoon baking powder
- 1 teaspoon paprika
- 1/2 teaspoon garlic powder
- Salt and pepper to taste
- 1 cup sparkling water
- 1 tablespoon olive oil
- 2 large sweet potatoes, cut into fries
- Fresh parsley for garnish
- Lemon wedges for serving

### Instructions:

1. **Prepare the Sweet Potato Fries:**
    - Preheat the oven to 425°F (220°C). Toss sweet potato fries in olive oil, salt, and pepper. Spread them out on a baking sheet and bake for 25-30 minutes, flipping halfway through.
2. **Make the Batter:**
    - In a bowl, mix flour, baking powder, paprika, garlic powder, salt, and pepper. Slowly add sparkling water to make a smooth batter.
3. **Cook the Fish:**
    - Dip fish fillets in the batter, then fry in hot oil over medium heat for 3-4 minutes per side, until golden and crispy.
4. **Serve:**
    - Serve the fish with sweet potato fries, garnished with parsley and lemon wedges.

**Grilled Swordfish with Mango Salsa**

## Ingredients:

- 4 swordfish steaks
- 1 tablespoon olive oil
- 1 teaspoon smoked paprika
- Salt and pepper to taste
- 1 mango, peeled and diced
- 1/4 cup red onion, diced
- 1/4 cup cilantro, chopped
- 1 tablespoon lime juice

## Instructions:

1. **Prepare the Swordfish:**
    - Preheat the grill to medium-high heat. Brush swordfish steaks with olive oil and season with smoked paprika, salt, and pepper.
2. **Grill the Swordfish:**
    - Grill swordfish for 4-5 minutes per side until cooked through.
3. **Make the Mango Salsa:**
    - In a bowl, combine mango, red onion, cilantro, and lime juice. Season with salt and pepper.
4. **Serve:**
    - Top grilled swordfish with mango salsa and serve immediately.

**Salmon Burger with Spicy Aioli**

## Ingredients:

- 1 lb fresh salmon, skin removed, finely chopped
- 1/4 cup breadcrumbs
- 1 egg
- 1 tablespoon Dijon mustard
- 1 teaspoon lemon zest
- Salt and pepper to taste
- 4 burger buns
- Lettuce and tomato slices for topping

## For the Spicy Aioli:

- 1/4 cup mayonnaise
- 1 tablespoon sriracha sauce
- 1 teaspoon lemon juice
- 1 teaspoon garlic, minced

## Instructions:

1. **Make the Salmon Patties:**
    - In a bowl, combine chopped salmon, breadcrumbs, egg, Dijon mustard, lemon zest, salt, and pepper. Mix well and form into 4 patties.
2. **Cook the Patties:**
    - Heat a skillet or grill pan over medium-high heat. Cook the patties for 4-5 minutes per side, until golden and cooked through.
3. **Prepare the Aioli:**
    - In a small bowl, combine mayonnaise, sriracha, lemon juice, and garlic. Mix until smooth.
4. **Assemble the Burger:**
    - Toast the burger buns and spread spicy aioli on the bottom bun. Top with the salmon patty, lettuce, and tomato. Serve immediately.

**Baked Cod with Cherry Tomatoes**

**Ingredients:**

- 4 cod fillets
- 1 pint cherry tomatoes, halved
- 2 cloves garlic, minced
- 2 tablespoons olive oil
- 1 teaspoon dried oregano
- Salt and pepper to taste
- Fresh parsley for garnish

**Instructions:**

1. **Preheat the Oven:**
   - Preheat the oven to 375°F (190°C). Place cod fillets on a baking sheet lined with parchment paper.
2. **Prepare the Vegetables:**
   - In a bowl, combine cherry tomatoes, garlic, olive oil, oregano, salt, and pepper. Spread the tomatoes around the fish fillets.
3. **Bake:**
   - Bake for 12-15 minutes, or until the cod is opaque and flakes easily.
4. **Serve:**
   - Garnish with fresh parsley and serve with rice or roasted vegetables.

**Shrimp Stir-Fry with Vegetables**

**Ingredients:**

- 1 lb shrimp, peeled and deveined
- 2 tablespoons olive oil
- 1 red bell pepper, sliced
- 1 yellow bell pepper, sliced
- 1 zucchini, sliced
- 1 onion, sliced
- 2 cloves garlic, minced
- 2 tablespoons soy sauce
- 1 tablespoon sesame oil
- 1 tablespoon honey
- Sesame seeds for garnish
- Fresh cilantro for garnish

**Instructions:**

1. **Cook the Shrimp:**
    - Heat olive oil in a large skillet or wok over medium-high heat. Add shrimp and cook for 2-3 minutes on each side until pink and opaque. Remove from the skillet.
2. **Stir-Fry the Vegetables:**
    - In the same skillet, add a bit more oil if needed. Stir-fry the bell peppers, zucchini, onion, and garlic for 3-4 minutes until tender.
3. **Make the Sauce:**
    - In a small bowl, whisk together soy sauce, sesame oil, and honey. Add this to the skillet with the vegetables and stir well.
4. **Combine:**
    - Return the cooked shrimp to the skillet and toss everything together to combine.
5. **Serve:**
    - Garnish with sesame seeds and cilantro. Serve with steamed rice or noodles.

**Sushi Rolls with Sustainable Fish**

**Ingredients:**

- 2 cups sushi rice, cooked and cooled
- 4 sheets nori (seaweed)
- 1/2 lb sushi-grade tuna or salmon, thinly sliced
- 1 avocado, sliced
- 1 cucumber, julienned
- Soy sauce for dipping
- Pickled ginger for serving
- Wasabi for serving

**Instructions:**

1. **Prepare the Sushi Rolls:**
    - Lay a sheet of nori on a bamboo sushi mat. Spread a thin layer of sushi rice over the nori, leaving a 1-inch border at the top.
2. **Add the Fillings:**
    - Place slices of tuna or salmon, avocado, and cucumber in a line across the center of the rice.
3. **Roll the Sushi:**
    - Using the sushi mat, carefully roll the sushi away from you, pressing lightly to form a tight roll.
4. **Slice and Serve:**
    - Slice the roll into 6-8 pieces using a sharp knife. Serve with soy sauce, pickled ginger, and wasabi.

**Octopus Salad with Olive Oil and Lemon**

**Ingredients:**

- 1 lb octopus, cooked and cut into bite-sized pieces
- 1/4 cup olive oil
- 2 tablespoons fresh lemon juice
- 1 tablespoon fresh parsley, chopped
- 1 teaspoon capers
- Salt and pepper to taste

**Instructions:**

1. **Prepare the Octopus:**
    - If the octopus is not pre-cooked, boil it in salted water for about 45 minutes, until tender. Allow it to cool and then cut into bite-sized pieces.
2. **Assemble the Salad:**
    - In a large bowl, combine octopus, olive oil, lemon juice, parsley, and capers. Toss gently to combine.
3. **Serve:**
    - Season with salt and pepper, then serve chilled or at room temperature.

**Fish Tacos with Cabbage Slaw**

**Ingredients:**

- 1 lb white fish fillets (such as cod or tilapia)
- 1 tablespoon olive oil
- 1 teaspoon chili powder
- 1/2 teaspoon cumin
- Salt and pepper to taste
- 8 small corn tortillas
- 1 cup shredded cabbage
- 1/4 cup cilantro, chopped
- 1/4 cup lime juice
- 1/4 cup sour cream
- Hot sauce (optional)

**Instructions:**

1. **Cook the Fish:**
    - Heat olive oil in a skillet over medium-high heat. Season fish fillets with chili powder, cumin, salt, and pepper. Cook the fish for 3-4 minutes per side, until golden and cooked through. Flake the fish into pieces.
2. **Make the Cabbage Slaw:**
    - In a bowl, combine shredded cabbage, cilantro, lime juice, and sour cream. Mix well.
3. **Assemble the Tacos:**
    - Warm the tortillas and fill each with a portion of the fish and top with cabbage slaw. Add hot sauce if desired.
4. **Serve:**
    - Serve with lime wedges on the side.

**Grilled Mahi-Mahi with Pineapple Salsa**

**Ingredients:**

- 4 mahi-mahi fillets
- 2 tablespoons olive oil
- 1 teaspoon paprika
- Salt and pepper to taste
- 1 cup pineapple, diced
- 1/4 cup red onion, diced
- 1/4 cup cilantro, chopped
- 1 tablespoon lime juice

**Instructions:**

1. **Grill the Mahi-Mahi:**
   - Preheat the grill to medium-high heat. Brush mahi-mahi fillets with olive oil and season with paprika, salt, and pepper. Grill for 4-5 minutes per side, until cooked through.
2. **Make the Pineapple Salsa:**
   - In a bowl, combine diced pineapple, red onion, cilantro, and lime juice. Stir gently.
3. **Serve:**
   - Top the grilled mahi-mahi with the pineapple salsa and serve immediately.

**Seaweed Salad with Sesame Dressing**

**Ingredients:**

- 1 cup dried seaweed (wakame or kombu)
- 2 tablespoons rice vinegar
- 1 tablespoon soy sauce
- 1 tablespoon sesame oil
- 1 teaspoon sugar
- 1 teaspoon sesame seeds
- 1 teaspoon grated ginger

**Instructions:**

1. **Rehydrate the Seaweed:**
    - Soak dried seaweed in warm water for about 10 minutes until softened. Drain and set aside.
2. **Make the Dressing:**
    - In a bowl, whisk together rice vinegar, soy sauce, sesame oil, sugar, and grated ginger.
3. **Assemble the Salad:**
    - Toss the rehydrated seaweed with the sesame dressing. Garnish with sesame seeds.
4. **Serve:**
    - Serve chilled as a side dish or light appetizer.

**Salmon and Avocado Sushi Bowls**

**Ingredients:**

- 1 lb sushi-grade salmon, diced
- 1 cup sushi rice, cooked and cooled
- 1 avocado, sliced
- 1/4 cup cucumber, sliced
- 1/4 cup soy sauce
- 1 tablespoon sesame oil
- 1 tablespoon rice vinegar
- 1 teaspoon sesame seeds
- Pickled ginger for serving

**Instructions:**

1. **Prepare the Salmon:**
    - Cube the sushi-grade salmon and place it in a bowl. Drizzle with soy sauce, sesame oil, and rice vinegar. Let marinate for 10-15 minutes.
2. **Assemble the Bowl:**
    - Divide the cooked rice into bowls. Top with marinated salmon, avocado, cucumber, and sesame seeds.
3. **Serve:**
    - Serve with pickled ginger on the side. Enjoy immediately.

# Shrimp and Zucchini Noodles

## Ingredients:

- 1 lb shrimp, peeled and deveined
- 4 zucchini, spiralized into noodles
- 2 cloves garlic, minced
- 2 tablespoons olive oil
- 1 tablespoon lemon juice
- 1 teaspoon chili flakes (optional)
- Salt and pepper to taste
- Fresh parsley for garnish

## Instructions:

1. **Cook the Shrimp:**
   - Heat olive oil in a large skillet over medium-high heat. Add shrimp and garlic, cooking for 2-3 minutes per side until pink and cooked through. Remove from the skillet and set aside.
2. **Prepare the Zucchini Noodles:**
   - In the same skillet, add the spiralized zucchini noodles. Cook for 2-3 minutes until tender, but still al dente.
3. **Combine:**
   - Add the cooked shrimp back to the skillet with the zucchini noodles. Stir in lemon juice, chili flakes (if using), and season with salt and pepper.
4. **Serve:**
   - Garnish with fresh parsley and serve immediately.

**Baked Salmon with Mustard and Herb Crust**

**Ingredients:**

- 4 salmon fillets
- 2 tablespoons Dijon mustard
- 1 tablespoon olive oil
- 1/4 cup breadcrumbs
- 2 tablespoons fresh parsley, chopped
- 1 tablespoon fresh dill, chopped
- 1 teaspoon lemon zest
- Salt and pepper to taste

**Instructions:**

1. **Preheat the Oven:**
    - Preheat the oven to 375°F (190°C). Line a baking sheet with parchment paper.
2. **Prepare the Mustard and Herb Crust:**
    - In a bowl, combine Dijon mustard, olive oil, breadcrumbs, parsley, dill, lemon zest, salt, and pepper. Mix until well combined.
3. **Prepare the Salmon:**
    - Place the salmon fillets on the prepared baking sheet. Spread the mustard and herb mixture evenly on top of each fillet.
4. **Bake:**
    - Bake for 12-15 minutes, or until the salmon is cooked through and flakes easily with a fork.
5. **Serve:**
    - Serve immediately with a side of vegetables or a salad.

**Fish Stew with Fresh Tomatoes**

**Ingredients:**

- 1 lb white fish fillets (such as cod or tilapia), cut into chunks
- 2 tablespoons olive oil
- 1 onion, chopped
- 3 cloves garlic, minced
- 2 cups fresh tomatoes, chopped
- 1 cup vegetable broth
- 1 teaspoon paprika
- 1/2 teaspoon thyme
- 1/2 teaspoon chili flakes (optional)
- Salt and pepper to taste
- Fresh basil for garnish

**Instructions:**

1. **Prepare the Stew Base:**
   - Heat olive oil in a large pot over medium heat. Add the onion and garlic and sauté until soft and fragrant, about 5 minutes.
2. **Add Tomatoes and Seasonings:**
   - Stir in the chopped tomatoes, vegetable broth, paprika, thyme, and chili flakes (if using). Bring to a simmer and cook for 10 minutes, allowing the flavors to meld.
3. **Add Fish:**
   - Add the fish chunks to the pot, season with salt and pepper, and simmer for another 10-12 minutes, or until the fish is cooked through.
4. **Serve:**
   - Garnish with fresh basil and serve with crusty bread or rice.

**Sea Bass with Roasted Vegetables**

**Ingredients:**

- 4 sea bass fillets
- 1 tablespoon olive oil
- 2 cups mixed vegetables (carrots, bell peppers, zucchini), chopped
- 1 teaspoon dried thyme
- 1 teaspoon paprika
- Salt and pepper to taste
- Lemon wedges for serving

**Instructions:**

1. **Preheat the Oven:**
    - Preheat the oven to 400°F (200°C). Line a baking sheet with parchment paper.
2. **Prepare the Roasted Vegetables:**
    - Toss the chopped vegetables with olive oil, thyme, paprika, salt, and pepper. Spread evenly on the baking sheet.
3. **Roast Vegetables:**
    - Roast the vegetables for 20-25 minutes, or until tender and lightly browned.
4. **Cook the Sea Bass:**
    - While the vegetables are roasting, season the sea bass fillets with salt and pepper. Heat a skillet over medium-high heat with olive oil and cook the fish for 3-4 minutes per side, until golden and cooked through.
5. **Serve:**
    - Serve the sea bass fillets on a bed of roasted vegetables with lemon wedges.

**Grilled Shrimp Skewers with Garlic and Lemon**

**Ingredients:**

- 1 lb shrimp, peeled and deveined
- 2 cloves garlic, minced
- 2 tablespoons olive oil
- 1 tablespoon lemon juice
- 1 teaspoon lemon zest
- Salt and pepper to taste
- Fresh parsley for garnish

**Instructions:**

1. **Marinate the Shrimp:**
     - In a bowl, combine garlic, olive oil, lemon juice, lemon zest, salt, and pepper. Add the shrimp and toss to coat. Let marinate for 15-20 minutes.
2. **Grill the Shrimp:**
     - Preheat the grill to medium-high heat. Thread the shrimp onto skewers and grill for 2-3 minutes per side, until pink and cooked through.
3. **Serve:**
     - Garnish with fresh parsley and serve with a side of rice or a salad.

**Spicy Tuna Salad**

**Ingredients:**

- 1 lb sushi-grade tuna, cubed
- 2 tablespoons mayonnaise
- 1 tablespoon sriracha sauce
- 1 teaspoon soy sauce
- 1 tablespoon sesame oil
- 1 tablespoon lime juice
- 1 teaspoon sesame seeds
- 1/4 cup scallions, chopped
- 1/4 cup cucumber, julienned

**Instructions:**

1. **Prepare the Tuna:**
   - In a bowl, combine tuna, mayonnaise, sriracha, soy sauce, sesame oil, and lime juice. Mix gently to coat.
2. **Add Garnishes:**
   - Stir in sesame seeds, scallions, and cucumber.
3. **Serve:**
   - Serve the spicy tuna salad over a bed of greens, with rice, or as a filling for sushi rolls.

**Mackerel with Roasted Potatoes and Kale**

**Ingredients:**

- 4 mackerel fillets
- 2 tablespoons olive oil
- 1 lb baby potatoes, halved
- 2 cups kale, chopped
- 1 teaspoon paprika
- 1 tablespoon lemon juice
- Salt and pepper to taste

**Instructions:**

1. **Roast the Potatoes:**
    - Preheat the oven to 400°F (200°C). Toss the halved potatoes with olive oil, paprika, salt, and pepper. Spread on a baking sheet and roast for 25-30 minutes, until tender.
2. **Cook the Mackerel:**
    - While the potatoes are roasting, season the mackerel fillets with salt, pepper, and lemon juice. Heat olive oil in a skillet over medium-high heat and cook the mackerel for 4-5 minutes per side until crispy and golden.
3. **Prepare the Kale:**
    - In the same skillet, add chopped kale and cook for 2-3 minutes until wilted.
4. **Serve:**
    - Serve the mackerel with roasted potatoes and sautéed kale.

**Coconut-Curry Fish Stew**

**Ingredients:**

- 1 lb white fish fillets, cut into chunks
- 1 can (14 oz) coconut milk
- 1 tablespoon red curry paste
- 1 onion, chopped
- 2 cloves garlic, minced
- 1 bell pepper, chopped
- 1 cup vegetable broth
- 1 teaspoon turmeric
- 1 tablespoon lime juice
- Fresh cilantro for garnish
- Salt and pepper to taste

**Instructions:**

1. **Prepare the Stew Base:**
   - In a large pot, heat olive oil over medium heat. Add onion and garlic, cooking until softened, about 5 minutes. Stir in curry paste, turmeric, and bell pepper.
2. **Add Coconut Milk and Broth:**
   - Pour in the coconut milk and vegetable broth. Bring to a simmer and cook for 10 minutes.
3. **Add Fish:**
   - Add the fish chunks to the pot and cook for 8-10 minutes, until the fish is cooked through.
4. **Finish and Serve:**
   - Stir in lime juice and season with salt and pepper. Garnish with fresh cilantro and serve with rice or naan.

# Poke Salad with Ahi Tuna

## Ingredients:

- 1 lb ahi tuna, cubed
- 2 cups mixed greens
- 1/2 cucumber, thinly sliced
- 1/2 avocado, diced
- 1/4 cup edamame, cooked
- 1 tablespoon soy sauce
- 1 tablespoon sesame oil
- 1 tablespoon rice vinegar
- 1 teaspoon sriracha sauce (optional)
- 1 tablespoon sesame seeds
- 1/4 cup scallions, chopped
- Lemon wedges for garnish

## Instructions:

1. **Marinate the Tuna:**
   - In a bowl, combine the ahi tuna with soy sauce, sesame oil, rice vinegar, and sriracha (if using). Mix gently and let marinate for 10-15 minutes.
2. **Prepare the Salad:**
   - In a large bowl, toss the mixed greens, cucumber, avocado, edamame, and scallions.
3. **Assemble the Poke Salad:**
   - Top the salad with the marinated tuna and sprinkle with sesame seeds.
4. **Serve:**
   - Serve immediately with lemon wedges on the side.

**Blackened Tilapia with Avocado**

**Ingredients:**

- 4 tilapia fillets
- 2 tablespoons blackened seasoning
- 1 tablespoon olive oil
- 1 avocado, sliced
- 1/2 lime, juiced
- Fresh cilantro for garnish
- Salt and pepper to taste

**Instructions:**

1. **Prepare the Tilapia:**
    - Sprinkle the blackened seasoning evenly over both sides of the tilapia fillets.
2. **Cook the Tilapia:**
    - Heat olive oil in a skillet over medium-high heat. Cook the tilapia fillets for 3-4 minutes per side, until the fish is cooked through and has a crispy, blackened crust.
3. **Prepare the Avocado:**
    - While the fish is cooking, slice the avocado and squeeze fresh lime juice over the slices.
4. **Serve:**
    - Serve the blackened tilapia with the avocado slices on top. Garnish with fresh cilantro and season with salt and pepper.

**Grilled Sardines with Garlic and Lemon**

**Ingredients:**

- 8-10 sardines, cleaned and gutted
- 2 tablespoons olive oil
- 2 cloves garlic, minced
- 1 lemon, thinly sliced
- 1 teaspoon fresh parsley, chopped
- Salt and pepper to taste

**Instructions:**

1. **Prepare the Sardines:**
   - Preheat the grill to medium-high heat. Brush the sardines with olive oil and season with salt and pepper.
2. **Grill the Sardines:**
   - Grill the sardines for 2-3 minutes per side until they are golden and cooked through.
3. **Prepare the Garlic and Lemon:**
   - While the sardines are grilling, sauté the garlic in olive oil over medium heat until fragrant, about 1 minute. Add the lemon slices and cook for another 2 minutes.
4. **Serve:**
   - Place the grilled sardines on a platter and drizzle with the garlic-lemon mixture. Garnish with fresh parsley and serve immediately.

**Baked Halibut with Pesto and Cherry Tomatoes**

**Ingredients:**

- 4 halibut fillets
- 1 cup pesto (store-bought or homemade)
- 1 pint cherry tomatoes, halved
- 1 tablespoon olive oil
- Salt and pepper to taste
- Fresh basil for garnish

**Instructions:**

1. **Preheat the Oven:**
   - Preheat the oven to 375°F (190°C).
2. **Prepare the Halibut:**
   - Place the halibut fillets on a baking sheet lined with parchment paper. Season with salt and pepper.
3. **Bake the Halibut:**
   - Spread a generous amount of pesto over each fillet and top with halved cherry tomatoes. Drizzle with olive oil. Bake for 12-15 minutes, or until the fish flakes easily with a fork.
4. **Serve:**
   - Garnish with fresh basil and serve with a side of rice or quinoa.

**Mussels in White Wine Sauce**

**Ingredients:**

- 2 lbs mussels, cleaned and debearded
- 1 tablespoon olive oil
- 3 cloves garlic, minced
- 1/2 cup dry white wine
- 1/2 cup vegetable broth
- 1/4 cup fresh parsley, chopped
- 1 tablespoon butter
- Salt and pepper to taste
- Lemon wedges for garnish

**Instructions:**

1. **Cook the Garlic:**
    - Heat olive oil in a large pot over medium heat. Add garlic and cook for 1-2 minutes, until fragrant.
2. **Add Wine and Broth:**
    - Pour in the white wine and vegetable broth. Bring to a simmer and cook for 2-3 minutes.
3. **Cook the Mussels:**
    - Add the mussels to the pot and cover. Cook for 5-7 minutes, or until the mussels have opened. Discard any mussels that do not open.
4. **Finish the Sauce:**
    - Stir in butter, fresh parsley, salt, and pepper. Mix gently.
5. **Serve:**
    - Serve the mussels in bowls with the white wine sauce. Garnish with lemon wedges.

**Shrimp Scampi with Whole Wheat Pasta**

## Ingredients:

- 1 lb shrimp, peeled and deveined
- 8 oz whole wheat spaghetti or linguine
- 4 cloves garlic, minced
- 1/4 cup olive oil
- 1/2 cup white wine
- 1 tablespoon lemon juice
- 1/4 teaspoon red pepper flakes
- Salt and pepper to taste
- Fresh parsley for garnish

## Instructions:

1. **Cook the Pasta:**
    - Cook the whole wheat pasta according to package instructions. Drain and set aside.
2. **Cook the Shrimp:**
    - In a large skillet, heat olive oil over medium-high heat. Add garlic and cook for 1 minute, until fragrant. Add shrimp and cook for 2-3 minutes per side until pink and cooked through.
3. **Make the Scampi Sauce:**
    - Add white wine, lemon juice, and red pepper flakes to the skillet. Let the sauce simmer for 2-3 minutes to reduce slightly. Season with salt and pepper.
4. **Combine Pasta and Shrimp:**
    - Add the cooked pasta to the skillet and toss to coat in the sauce.
5. **Serve:**
    - Garnish with fresh parsley and serve immediately.

**Salmon with Quinoa and Roasted Veggies**

**Ingredients:**

- 4 salmon fillets
- 1 cup quinoa
- 2 cups mixed vegetables (such as zucchini, bell peppers, and cherry tomatoes), chopped
- 2 tablespoons olive oil
- 1 teaspoon dried thyme
- Salt and pepper to taste
- Lemon wedges for serving

**Instructions:**

1. **Preheat the Oven:**
    - Preheat the oven to 400°F (200°C). Line a baking sheet with parchment paper.
2. **Roast the Vegetables:**
    - Toss the chopped vegetables with olive oil, dried thyme, salt, and pepper. Roast for 20-25 minutes, until tender and slightly browned.
3. **Cook the Quinoa:**
    - In a medium pot, cook the quinoa according to package instructions.
4. **Cook the Salmon:**
    - While the vegetables are roasting, season the salmon fillets with salt and pepper. Heat olive oil in a skillet over medium-high heat and cook the salmon for 3-4 minutes per side until golden and cooked through.
5. **Serve:**
    - Serve the salmon on a bed of quinoa with the roasted vegetables. Garnish with lemon wedges.

**Fish Tacos with Cilantro Lime Dressing**

**Ingredients:**

- 1 lb white fish fillets (such as cod or tilapia)
- 8 small corn tortillas
- 1 cup shredded cabbage
- 1 avocado, sliced
- 1/4 cup fresh cilantro, chopped
- 1/4 cup Greek yogurt
- 1 tablespoon lime juice
- 1 teaspoon chili powder
- Salt and pepper to taste
- Olive oil for cooking

**Instructions:**

1. **Cook the Fish:**
   - Heat olive oil in a skillet over medium heat. Season the fish fillets with chili powder, salt, and pepper. Cook for 3-4 minutes per side, until the fish flakes easily with a fork.
2. **Prepare the Cilantro Lime Dressing:**
   - In a small bowl, mix Greek yogurt, lime juice, and fresh cilantro. Season with salt and pepper.
3. **Assemble the Tacos:**
   - Warm the tortillas in a dry skillet. Flake the cooked fish into pieces and place on the tortillas. Top with shredded cabbage, avocado slices, and cilantro lime dressing.
4. **Serve:**
   - Serve the fish tacos immediately, garnished with extra cilantro.

**Seared Tuna with Cucumber and Sesame**

**Ingredients:**

- 2 ahi tuna steaks
- 1 tablespoon sesame oil
- 1 cucumber, thinly sliced
- 1 tablespoon soy sauce
- 1 tablespoon rice vinegar
- 1 teaspoon sesame seeds
- 1/4 teaspoon wasabi (optional)
- Salt and pepper to taste

**Instructions:**

1. **Sear the Tuna:**
    - Heat sesame oil in a skillet over high heat. Season the tuna steaks with salt and pepper. Sear the tuna for 1-2 minutes per side for rare, or longer for desired doneness.
2. **Prepare the Cucumber:**
    - While the tuna is searing, mix the cucumber slices with soy sauce, rice vinegar, and sesame seeds.
3. **Serve:**
    - Slice the seared tuna and arrange it on a plate. Serve with the cucumber salad and a touch of wasabi, if desired.

**Clam Chowder with a Healthy Twist**

**Ingredients:**

- 2 lbs fresh clams, cleaned and shelled (or canned clams)
- 1 tablespoon olive oil
- 1 medium onion, chopped
- 2 cloves garlic, minced
- 2 large potatoes, peeled and diced
- 4 cups low-sodium vegetable broth
- 1 cup unsweetened almond milk (or skim milk)
- 1 cup corn kernels (fresh or frozen)
- 1 teaspoon thyme
- Salt and pepper to taste
- Fresh parsley for garnish

**Instructions:**

1. **Prepare the Clams:**
   - If using fresh clams, steam them in a large pot until they open, about 5-7 minutes. Remove the clams, discard any that do not open, and set aside. If using canned clams, drain and set aside.
2. **Sauté Vegetables:**
   - In a large pot, heat olive oil over medium heat. Add onion and garlic and sauté for 2-3 minutes until softened.
3. **Make the Chowder Base:**
   - Add the diced potatoes, vegetable broth, almond milk, and thyme to the pot. Bring to a boil, then reduce heat and simmer for 10-12 minutes until the potatoes are tender.
4. **Add Corn and Clams:**
   - Stir in the corn kernels and clams. Continue cooking for another 5-7 minutes, ensuring the clams are heated through.
5. **Season and Serve:**
   - Season with salt and pepper to taste. Garnish with fresh parsley and serve hot.

**Grilled Salmon with Roasted Asparagus**

**Ingredients:**

- 4 salmon fillets
- 1 bunch asparagus, trimmed
- 2 tablespoons olive oil, divided
- 1 teaspoon lemon zest
- 1 tablespoon lemon juice
- 1 teaspoon garlic powder
- Salt and pepper to taste
- Fresh dill for garnish

**Instructions:**

1. **Prepare the Salmon:**
    - Preheat the grill to medium-high heat. Drizzle the salmon fillets with 1 tablespoon olive oil, lemon juice, garlic powder, salt, and pepper.
2. **Grill the Salmon:**
    - Place the salmon fillets on the grill, skin-side down, and cook for 4-5 minutes per side, or until the salmon flakes easily with a fork.
3. **Prepare the Asparagus:**
    - Preheat the oven to 400°F (200°C). Place the asparagus on a baking sheet, drizzle with the remaining olive oil, and season with salt and pepper. Roast for 15-20 minutes, or until tender and slightly crispy.
4. **Serve:**
    - Serve the grilled salmon alongside the roasted asparagus, garnished with lemon zest and fresh dill.

**Pappardelle with Clams and Garlic**

**Ingredients:**

- 8 oz pappardelle pasta
- 2 cups fresh clams (or canned clams)
- 4 cloves garlic, minced
- 1 tablespoon olive oil
- 1/2 cup dry white wine
- 1/4 cup fresh parsley, chopped
- 1 tablespoon lemon juice
- Salt and pepper to taste

**Instructions:**

1. **Cook the Pappardelle:**
   - Cook the pappardelle pasta according to package instructions, then drain and set aside.
2. **Cook the Clams:**
   - In a large skillet, heat olive oil over medium heat. Add garlic and sauté for 1-2 minutes until fragrant. Add the clams and white wine. Cover and cook for 5-7 minutes, or until the clams open.
3. **Toss with Pasta:**
   - Add the cooked pasta to the skillet with the clams. Toss gently to combine, then stir in lemon juice and fresh parsley.
4. **Serve:**
   - Season with salt and pepper to taste and serve immediately.

**Baked Fish with Herb-Crusted Potatoes**

**Ingredients:**

- 4 white fish fillets (such as cod or tilapia)
- 2 large russet potatoes, thinly sliced
- 2 tablespoons olive oil
- 1 teaspoon dried thyme
- 1 teaspoon rosemary, chopped
- 1 tablespoon fresh parsley, chopped
- 1 lemon, sliced
- Salt and pepper to taste

**Instructions:**

1. **Preheat the Oven:**
   - Preheat the oven to 375°F (190°C). Line a baking sheet with parchment paper.
2. **Prepare the Potatoes:**
   - Toss the potato slices with olive oil, thyme, rosemary, salt, and pepper. Spread them out evenly on the baking sheet and bake for 25-30 minutes, flipping halfway through, until golden and crispy.
3. **Prepare the Fish:**
   - While the potatoes are baking, season the fish fillets with salt and pepper. Place them on a separate baking sheet and top with lemon slices. Bake for 12-15 minutes, or until the fish flakes easily with a fork.
4. **Serve:**
   - Serve the baked fish alongside the herb-crusted potatoes and garnish with fresh parsley.

**Crab Cakes with Lemon-Dijon Aioli**

**Ingredients:**

- 1 lb lump crab meat
- 1/4 cup breadcrumbs
- 1 egg, beaten
- 1 tablespoon Dijon mustard
- 2 tablespoons mayonnaise
- 1 teaspoon Old Bay seasoning
- 1 tablespoon fresh parsley, chopped
- 2 tablespoons olive oil
- For Aioli: 1/4 cup mayonnaise, 1 tablespoon Dijon mustard, 1 tablespoon lemon juice, and salt

**Instructions:**

1. **Prepare the Crab Cakes:**
    - In a bowl, combine crab meat, breadcrumbs, beaten egg, Dijon mustard, mayonnaise, Old Bay seasoning, and parsley. Form the mixture into small cakes.
2. **Cook the Crab Cakes:**
    - Heat olive oil in a skillet over medium heat. Cook the crab cakes for 3-4 minutes per side, until golden and crispy.
3. **Make the Aioli:**
    - In a small bowl, whisk together mayonnaise, Dijon mustard, lemon juice, and salt until smooth.
4. **Serve:**
    - Serve the crab cakes with a side of lemon-Dijon aioli for dipping.

**Sautéed Fish with Zucchini and Tomatoes**

**Ingredients:**

- 4 fish fillets (such as sole or cod)
- 2 zucchinis, sliced
- 1 pint cherry tomatoes, halved
- 2 tablespoons olive oil
- 2 cloves garlic, minced
- 1 teaspoon fresh basil, chopped
- Salt and pepper to taste

**Instructions:**

1. **Cook the Fish:**
    - Heat olive oil in a skillet over medium-high heat. Season the fish fillets with salt and pepper and cook for 3-4 minutes per side, until golden and cooked through. Remove the fish and set aside.
2. **Sauté the Vegetables:**
    - In the same skillet, add garlic and zucchini slices. Cook for 2-3 minutes until tender. Add the cherry tomatoes and cook for another 2 minutes until they soften.
3. **Serve:**
    - Return the fish to the skillet and sprinkle with fresh basil. Serve immediately.

**Salmon and Avocado Salad**

**Ingredients:**

- 4 salmon fillets
- 2 avocados, sliced
- 4 cups mixed greens
- 1/2 cucumber, sliced
- 1/4 red onion, thinly sliced
- 1 tablespoon olive oil
- 1 tablespoon balsamic vinegar
- Salt and pepper to taste

**Instructions:**

1. **Cook the Salmon:**
    - Heat olive oil in a skillet over medium-high heat. Season the salmon fillets with salt and pepper and cook for 3-4 minutes per side until golden and cooked through.
2. **Prepare the Salad:**
    - In a large bowl, toss the mixed greens, cucumber, onion, and avocado slices.
3. **Dress the Salad:**
    - Drizzle balsamic vinegar over the salad and toss gently to combine.
4. **Serve:**
    - Top the salad with the cooked salmon fillets and serve immediately.

**Grilled Squid with Lemon and Parsley**

**Ingredients:**

- 1 lb squid, cleaned and cut into rings
- 2 tablespoons olive oil
- 2 cloves garlic, minced
- 1 tablespoon fresh parsley, chopped
- 1 lemon, juiced
- Salt and pepper to taste

**Instructions:**

1. **Prepare the Squid:**
    - Preheat the grill to medium-high heat. Toss the squid rings with olive oil, garlic, salt, and pepper.
2. **Grill the Squid:**
    - Grill the squid for 2-3 minutes per side, until tender and slightly charred.
3. **Serve:**
    - Drizzle with fresh lemon juice and garnish with chopped parsley. Serve immediately.

**Shrimp and Mango Salad**

**Ingredients:**

- 1 lb cooked shrimp, peeled and deveined
- 1 ripe mango, diced
- 1 avocado, diced
- 2 cups mixed greens (arugula, spinach, or lettuce)
- 1/2 cucumber, thinly sliced
- 1/4 red onion, thinly sliced
- 1/4 cup fresh cilantro, chopped
- 1 tablespoon olive oil
- 2 tablespoons lime juice
- Salt and pepper to taste

**Instructions:**

1. **Prepare the Salad:**
     - In a large bowl, combine the shrimp, mango, avocado, cucumber, red onion, and cilantro.
2. **Make the Dressing:**
     - In a small bowl, whisk together olive oil, lime juice, salt, and pepper.
3. **Toss the Salad:**
     - Drizzle the dressing over the salad and toss gently to combine.
4. **Serve:**
     - Serve immediately as a refreshing light meal or appetizer.

**Fish Curry with Coconut Milk**

**Ingredients:**

- 1 lb white fish fillets (such as cod or tilapia), cut into chunks
- 1 tablespoon olive oil
- 1 onion, chopped
- 2 cloves garlic, minced
- 1 tablespoon grated ginger
- 2 tablespoons curry powder
- 1 teaspoon turmeric
- 1 can (14 oz) coconut milk
- 1/2 cup vegetable broth
- 1 cup spinach, chopped
- 1 tablespoon lime juice
- Salt and pepper to taste
- Fresh cilantro for garnish

**Instructions:**

1. **Sauté the Aromatics:**
   - In a large pot, heat olive oil over medium heat. Add the onion, garlic, and ginger, and sauté for 2-3 minutes until fragrant.
2. **Add the Spices:**
   - Stir in the curry powder and turmeric, cooking for another 1 minute to bring out the flavors.
3. **Simmer the Curry:**
   - Add the coconut milk and vegetable broth to the pot. Bring to a simmer, then add the fish chunks and cook for 8-10 minutes, until the fish is cooked through.
4. **Add Spinach and Season:**
   - Stir in the spinach and cook until wilted. Add lime juice, salt, and pepper to taste.
5. **Serve:**
   - Garnish with fresh cilantro and serve hot with rice or naan.

**Tuna Salad with Olive Oil and Lemon**

**Ingredients:**

- 2 cans (5 oz each) tuna, drained
- 1/4 cup olive oil
- 2 tablespoons lemon juice
- 1 tablespoon Dijon mustard
- 1/4 red onion, finely chopped
- 2 hard-boiled eggs, chopped
- 2 tablespoons fresh parsley, chopped
- Salt and pepper to taste

**Instructions:**

1. **Combine Ingredients:**
   - In a large bowl, combine the tuna, olive oil, lemon juice, Dijon mustard, onion, eggs, and parsley.
2. **Season the Salad:**
   - Season with salt and pepper to taste, mixing well.
3. **Serve:**
   - Serve the tuna salad over greens or as a sandwich filling.

**Shrimp and Broccoli Stir-Fry**

**Ingredients:**

- 1 lb shrimp, peeled and deveined
- 2 cups broccoli florets
- 1 tablespoon olive oil
- 2 cloves garlic, minced
- 1/2 cup low-sodium soy sauce
- 1 tablespoon sesame oil
- 1 tablespoon honey
- 1 teaspoon fresh ginger, grated
- 2 tablespoons sesame seeds
- Cooked rice for serving

**Instructions:**

1. **Sauté Shrimp:**
    - In a large skillet or wok, heat olive oil over medium-high heat. Add the shrimp and cook for 2-3 minutes per side, until pink and cooked through. Remove the shrimp and set aside.
2. **Stir-Fry Vegetables:**
    - In the same skillet, add a little more oil if needed and sauté garlic and broccoli for 4-5 minutes, until tender-crisp.
3. **Make the Sauce:**
    - In a small bowl, whisk together soy sauce, sesame oil, honey, and ginger.
4. **Combine:**
    - Return the shrimp to the skillet and pour the sauce over the shrimp and broccoli. Toss to coat and cook for another 2-3 minutes until everything is heated through.
5. **Serve:**
    - Serve the stir-fry over cooked rice and sprinkle with sesame seeds.

**Grilled Fish with Herb Chimichurri**

**Ingredients:**

- 4 fish fillets (such as cod, tilapia, or halibut)
- 1/4 cup olive oil
- 1/4 cup fresh parsley, chopped
- 2 tablespoons fresh oregano, chopped
- 2 tablespoons red wine vinegar
- 2 cloves garlic, minced
- 1/2 teaspoon red pepper flakes
- Salt and pepper to taste
- Lemon wedges for serving

**Instructions:**

1. **Prepare the Chimichurri:**
   - In a bowl, combine olive oil, parsley, oregano, vinegar, garlic, red pepper flakes, salt, and pepper. Mix well.
2. **Grill the Fish:**
   - Preheat the grill to medium-high heat. Season the fish fillets with salt and pepper. Grill for 3-4 minutes per side, or until the fish flakes easily with a fork.
3. **Serve:**
   - Spoon the herb chimichurri over the grilled fish and serve with lemon wedges.

**Roasted Sea Bass with Lemon and Capers**

## Ingredients:

- 2 sea bass fillets
- 1 tablespoon olive oil
- 1 lemon, sliced
- 2 tablespoons capers
- 1/4 cup fresh parsley, chopped
- Salt and pepper to taste

## Instructions:

1. **Preheat the Oven:**
    - Preheat the oven to 400°F (200°C). Line a baking sheet with parchment paper.
2. **Prepare the Sea Bass:**
    - Place the sea bass fillets on the prepared baking sheet. Drizzle with olive oil, and season with salt and pepper. Top with lemon slices and capers.
3. **Roast the Fish:**
    - Roast in the oven for 10-12 minutes, or until the fish flakes easily with a fork.
4. **Serve:**
    - Garnish with fresh parsley and serve with roasted vegetables or potatoes.

**Coconut Shrimp with Sweet Chili Sauce**

**Ingredients:**

- 1 lb large shrimp, peeled and deveined
- 1/2 cup shredded coconut
- 1/2 cup breadcrumbs
- 2 eggs, beaten
- 1/2 cup flour
- 1/4 teaspoon salt
- 1/4 teaspoon pepper
- 1/2 cup sweet chili sauce for dipping
- Vegetable oil for frying

**Instructions:**

1. **Prepare the Shrimp:**
    - Set up three shallow bowls: one with flour, one with beaten eggs, and one with a mixture of shredded coconut and breadcrumbs.
2. **Coat the Shrimp:**
    - Dip each shrimp into the flour, then the egg, and finally the coconut-breadcrumb mixture, pressing gently to coat.
3. **Fry the Shrimp:**
    - Heat vegetable oil in a skillet over medium heat. Fry the shrimp for 2-3 minutes per side, until golden brown and crispy.
4. **Serve:**
    - Serve the coconut shrimp with sweet chili sauce for dipping.

**Grilled Halibut with Lemon Butter Sauce**

**Ingredients:**

- 4 halibut fillets
- 2 tablespoons olive oil
- Salt and pepper to taste
- 1/4 cup butter
- 2 tablespoons fresh lemon juice
- 1 tablespoon fresh parsley, chopped
- Lemon wedges for serving

**Instructions:**

1. **Grill the Halibut:**
    - Preheat the grill to medium-high heat. Brush the halibut fillets with olive oil and season with salt and pepper. Grill for 4-5 minutes per side, or until the fish flakes easily with a fork.
2. **Make the Lemon Butter Sauce:**
    - In a small saucepan, melt the butter over low heat. Stir in lemon juice and fresh parsley.
3. **Serve:**
    - Drizzle the lemon butter sauce over the grilled halibut and serve with lemon wedges.

www.ingramcontent.com/pod-product-compliance
Lightning Source LLC
LaVergne TN
LVHW081342060526
838201LV00055B/2806